The Direction of
YOUR ERECTION

By He Who Rebels Against All

DANCE WITH ME BABY, DANCE WITH **AN ENTITY AS DARK+INSANE** AS ME
JUST FOR A NIGHT

ISBN 9781798168042
Fonts by Jess Latham.
Thank You.

Printed, Distributed and Bound in the United States of America
First Printing March 2019

Published by
He Who Rebels Against All
TreeHouse Publishing
Oklahoma City, Oklahoma

Thanks for getting a copy!
It really means the world to me.

The Direction of your ERECTION
By He Who Rebels Against All

EVERY sociologist and their mother has tried to take a shot at this.
Every preacher, philosopher, politician, psychologist
And everyone has missed the mark. Completely rapid misfires.

10,000 arrows from intense attempts and nobody hit that fucking
bullseye.

If they had, then I wouldn't have had to DO it.

What is homosexuality? What does it mean?
Aberration? Sin? Social Defect?

WRONG
NO
FAKE NEWS

none of y'all can aim for shit.

Jesus christ.

Give me the fucking bow.

I got this god damn thing.

takes aim

releases

smiles

I.OKAY.
So listen up. Drop your stupid ass rainbow flags and your bible verses right here.
Neither will be serving us. We don't need either of them.

sets them both on fire as the homosexual and the christian scream in shock

Deal with it. Because I need to you put all that other shit aside, and LISTEN to me for the next half hour.

Fellow homosexual - *you are guilty of making a total fool of yourself and thinking that wearing unicorn hats and being half naked was going to help push the gears of society forward. Society didn't need your naked body, it needed your mind. But you were too content to walk around with your ding dong obscenely out in the street, paired with stupid rainbow socks; making a "statement."*

Christian - *you're just guilty of not using ANY critical thinking on this, but I suppose in the spirit of your christ all can eventually be forgiven. Despite the fact that innumerable lives were lived out in shame and pain. Or far worse. All because of a book. If one book actually did all this damage, it'll take another (well written) one to UNDO it all.*

Both of you idiots have given me a headache.

Let's begin.

Being gay has NOTHING to do with what you think it has to do with.

Not the bible verses, not the scriptures, not "Sodom and Gomorrah."

None of that crap. NONE.

Here's the truth.

Hello...

Taps microphone

Is this thing on?

Looks at the horde of curious people, now watching
clears throat, self-consciously

This will be a defining contribution.
I leave something of monumental importance behind.

I'm suddenly at a strange point in my career as I write this; I'm transferring out of social sciences into the pure sciences (chemistry, biology, physics, astronomy) *but It's important that I make ONE last*

deposit to the contribution of sociology, my former field.
I'm exiting one door and preparing to open another.
I want to study the basic elements of this existence, vs. social pressure
and social structure of just one planet. Us, the Earth. Sociology studies
the variables of this planet's people. We've confirmed over 3,000 new
planets out there.
More interesting things abound than the mental issues of others. You can
see why I'm going into a different field. Desiring something less
emotional, and more intellectual.

As an official, soon-to-be scientist, I enjoy really elegant, mathematical
formulas to explain and model reality. I like to see sophistication in
simplification.
Taking hours and YEARS of hard work, boiled and condensed down to
just a few algebraic letters and numbers.
An expression, a theory that best describes the reality of a situation.
That is something to behold, especially when you understand exactly
what it is that you are seeing.

Taking these huge data sets, and giving a concise takeaway.
So, in keeping with the theme of simplicity (while concealing much
complicated jargon), I think it fitting it to explain something in a way that
it has never been explained before.

**After reading what I am about to say, homosexuality will
forever be easily explained away. F O R E V E R. That sentence
is in bold - but this is not just another bold claim.**
And a lot of the lingering issues that still surround it, will begin to
dissipate. Hopefully.
I need this to get filtered into the public water supply - without actually
watering any of it down - which is why I'll be keeping the price so cheap
and giving away as many free versions as I can.

I'll be throwing this book/paper at people's heads.

People need to hear this. Fuck the whole literary world. I'm not doing this to rub shoulders with the pulitzer prize winners.
This is for everyday people out there with gay family members and friends, acquaintances, etc... to understand.

What I am about to do - It's never been explained this way, which is why I'm taking this route.

The answer lies within the truth of these pages.

We're keeping it short, because we're ALREADY short for time.
The social damage and scarification has already been done in a million different forms. Now I have to clean up the *entire* **fucking mess**.

Speed, Efficiency, Thoroughness, Accuracy.
Lets do this quick, lets do it well, lets get it done, and lets get it done correctly, people. So we never have to do or say any of this AGAIN.

I'm not going to expound upon all the gay suicide, gay killing and bullying that has already happened, the LGBTQ-ABCDEFG Blah, blah blah bullshit
Or remark all that much on the Pulse shooting, hangings, all that fucked up stuff that's happened and been processed as history in American culture.

There is no use crying over spilt milk, or spilt souls.

I can't alter or amend the horror show of past, so it's best for brevity's sake to focus on the present moment and the moment leading into the future.

I CANT BRING BACK THE FUCKING DEAD

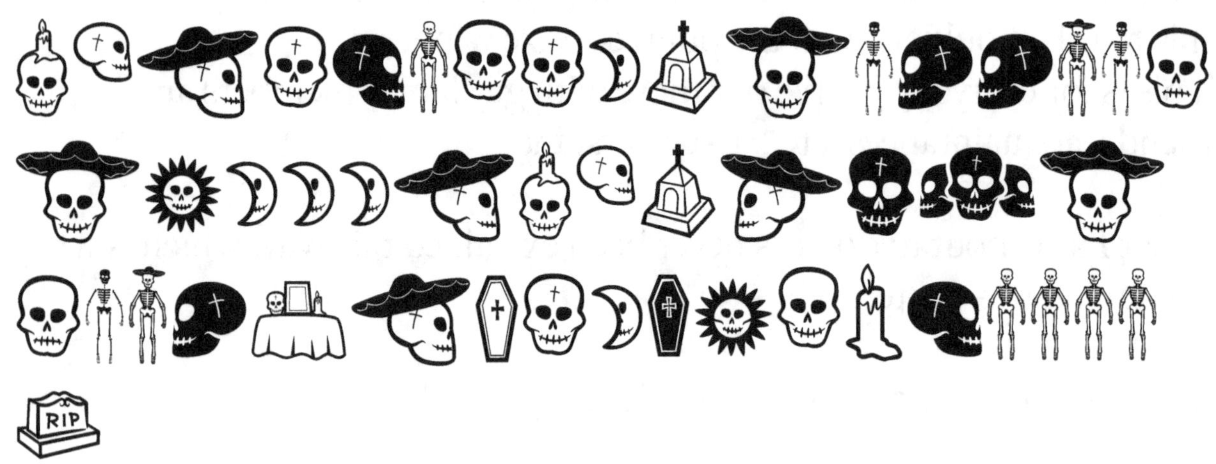

BUT I ALSO WONT LET HUMAN HISTORY
ANNE FRANK-ENSTEIN ME!

Before publishing this, years ago,
I wrote a 450 page book 11.5 x 8 (it looked like a HUGE phonebook),
complete with diagrams and poetry and any every other flavor of ideas I
had at the time,
to hit the issue from any possibly angle, it ended up hitting the Amazon
bestseller list for a week, and I was next to James Franco, a celebrity,
who was writing a poetry book about being gay.
A cool moment to see myself from, from the efforts of my own will and
stubbornness, succeeding on the publishing front, but writing isnt my
true calling,
even though I am writing now.
Dont ask, Dont Telephone.

SO! Here we go.

cracks knuckles

We all know what the Bible, (and also what every other religious text)
has to say on the subject.

Yes, Yes, yes eternal damnation, won't inherit the kingdom of god,
whipped by 1,000 demons, all that jazz

(all that jizz)

But the key to unlocking this forbidden door, has nothing to do with
Christianity, although Christianity is what has persecuted it and
preceded it.

It has nothing to do with the Bible, God, Moses, Jesus, Mohammed.

It has to do with my big, dangling WEINER.

*draws a penis on the chalkboard, complete with pubic hair AND
balls*
Stares at it for a second
Good enough

Let the record show that every other person that tried to tackle and give
diligence to this topic, tragically missed the mark by a fair margin.
That isn't to denigrate their work or ideas, at a wholesale level, but that
the undeniable truth hasn't ever been possessed so far by anyone in
history or any other sociological page.

We've been around (as a species) for about 200,000 years.
It's taken THAT long for someone to say this. It's so obvious it's painful
that it's been overlooked and hidden
for SO LONG.

We've gotten the hard stuff out of the way, so let me explain about other things that GET HARD.

erases the flaccid penis

Being gay, has nothing to do with what people THINK it has to do with.

No dances with lucifer at midnight, no sexual abuse,
No lack of strong, central male figures, no illuminati meetings (sadly, I wish)

It has nothing to do with the rainbow, or glitter, or unicorns, or anything prescribed.
There isn't anything wrong with that, but I do shake my head at the multitude of missteps that happened along the way to get up to this point,
when THIS point - meaning gay marriage and gay tolerance - could have been reached a far quicker rate with the aid of a cohesive and succinct message to stand behind,
instead of yelling and walking in a poorly sewn mermaid costume down the street and yelling *I WAS BORN THIS WAY.*

Fools. Born a damn fool. And then you tried doing all THAT stuff in front of "Born Again" Christians. Oh my god.

Of course being naked with your junk out - in a leather BDSM Harness - BACKFIRED.

*CHRIST ON A CROSS *Facepalms**

But then all the gays wonder why nobody took them and their cause seriously. CAUSE you look like pornography when you're trying to land something, politically (and even MORE importantly, philosophically.) DUR DUR DUR

You meant well, but you didn't succeed at the objective quite so well. You argued, you screamed, you ranted, you wrote your facebook posts, You still failed, because had you succeeded what lingered wouldn't still remain.

The problem, or the main problem, is that homosexuality, a sociological and sexual condition has become embedded, entwined and twisted into the battle of religious rhetoric,
which in itself has twisted itself even more.

Religion of the same idea can't even agree with ITSELF. It's why their are splits, schisms of thought and differing denominations. Take a completely unrelated issue and throw it into the mix - being gay - and you have a real fucking disaster waiting to unfold. Which it did.

Look how many strong and diverse opinions people have had on it.
People who aren't gay have had so much to say about it.
So much that was just flat out W R O N G.

Homosexuality is an issue in a layer of knots. It's always been

like a knotted up pair of headphones, wrapped in messy and
hard to remove layers of even more complicated knots.

But I'm untangling them, because even in 2019, there remain still many
knotted loops that surround the subject and twisted itself up even more.

I don't even need to argue about love, or feelings.
In fact, emotion can be taken right out of the equation on this.

This has never been put into print, it's never been talked about,
but here we go.

This is the simple, undeniable, incontrovertible truth.

ARE YOU READY? ARE YOU REALLY READY???

<u>My dick cannot get hard - looking at a naked woman.</u>

A vagina, a labia, a clitoris, doesn't move my wiener.
It will stay 3-4 inches and not grow if I look at one.
Even if I jerked off, I can't maintain an erection firm enough to finish.
That is literally IT.

So, barring all eternal death threats (which by the way are completely silly
and ultimately meaningless)
I can't get a stiffy looking at pictures of gravity losing tits and pussy.

Because I don't want to lick or flick or DICK down a clitoris... So I'm
going to hell.

Your "god" hates me because I don't wanna stare at some big ole' titties
or finger doodle a woman's labia box.

Dont wanna rub my manhood between a woman's fun bags. WOW.

You see how stupid that sounds.
It is really THAT SIMPLE, but you dumb dumbs have made it THAT
DIFFICULT on other people.

But people have taken their own life and been killed because they wont
put their wiener inside of a whoo-hah.

It sounds funny, but it's something dead serious
and too many good people are now dead because of it.

IMAGINARY GODS
have killed OFF REAL PEOPLE.

For example, there was a group of kids that took their own life for being
gay between 2011 - 2015 ish.
And for every month, another child who was gay, ended their life on
earth.

Go google it. Im not doing the legwork for you.
You can read their lives or not. It doesnt matter at this stage.
Kids writing these suicide notes about how they were sorry people were
ashamed of them and hanging themselves or blowing their brains out
with a gun they took.

We're not talking adults, we're talking young kids that hadn't even hit
age 16. 12 year olds.

Awful. And Terrible.

………..

So think about this, Going back to the dissertation on human attraction,
If I cant get hard looking at a cunt, or a twat, or whatever vulgar, crude,
rude word you want to refer to those anatomical parts as,
How am I going to have sex with said orifice, if thats all I need to do for
God to "love" me and be acceptable.

You cant fornicate someone with a soft cock.
 HELLO.
U CANT DRILL A HOLE
WITH A LIMP PYTHON

You can sure as hell try but thats gonna be awkward and laughable.

You really think your deity cares whether I have a pussaay or a cock in my
mouth?
Thats like saying the President is worried whether I have decaf or regular
coffee for breakfast.
I think God and the president have bigger things to worry about
and SPEAKING of big THINGS
So if I lick balls *which I have* Im going to spend the rest of my eternity
on fire.

Even if I was sorry - which I'm not - got down on my knees, prayed and
repented, held the rosary, I still wouldn't be able to bed a woman.

There is no moment in time - that is remotely possible - where I'm NOT
gay.

AND Do you really think God wants a homosexual man or ANY MAN
to subject himself to that kind of embarrassment and shame?

Trying to put it inside a chick's mound but it wont get up. REALLY???

Imagine the gayest man you've ever met, and then try and imagine him
going down on a female.
Yeah, it's not happening and WE BOTH know it.

You're dumb.
Like stupid dumb.
Not even funny dumb.
But more like you are a dumb-ass.

Me not getting hard for vagina, is seriously not a big deal at all, but its
been turned and made into the biggest HISTORICAL deal ever.

It has nothing to do with hating women - clearly not, since my own inner
circle has always been nothing but women.
It has nothing to do with not having a strong male figure in my life - I
grew up around politically incorrect NRA, Rodeo loving classically
masculine MEN
It has nothing to do with being abused, assaulted, ETC... Fill in the
blank with whatever crazy assertion,belief,idea thats been heard before.

The thing is, I can tell you exactly when I knew I was gay, before I
understood what that meant in society.

When I was six, I saw the naked statue of David. In an Encyclopedia.
(lol)
And I couldn't stop looking at his hanging phallus AND his marbled
Test-ickles
I was utterly captivated.
It was beautiful and whimsical and somehow powerful looking ALL at
the same time.

I knew I liked that from THAT age.

flaps wrist into the air GAY

The carnal, sexualized light went off then.

I knew, in that deep, type of KNOWING.

THEN When I was eight, when the internet was just taking off, I searched for "Big Hairy Wiener." Those exact words. Big. Hairy. Wiener.
I mean. LOL.
            ....MY DUDES I WAS ALWAYS GAY.

What Im saying is - in the least arrogant way I can - everything ANYONE has ever said or thought around this issue has been wrong, in so many different kinds of ways.

I cant get a boner for a bitch. Why should I even feel sorry or hate myself for that?

Big deal.
Big whoop.
Oh my GOD
WHO cares.
Get it through your SMALL brains.

Let's do this logically. Okay.

Seeing a dick makes my dick HARD, which would make my boyfriends dick HARD, because he likes dick too.

Its not that HARD 2 UNDERSTAND.

It really has nothing to do with ass, although thats where everyone gets hung up on,
and I didnt need to make an ass of myself to explain all of this.

If you put a photo of a woman in front of me, better yet,
If an actual naked woman was standing before me - the most physically perfect and beautiful lady ever - great tits, round ass, aesthetically beautiful face and hair, never seen a double cheeseburger before, perfect figure, I STILL wouldnt be salivating and struggling to control myself like a straight man.

Nothing would be happening inside my head or inside my blood vessels of my other head.

Nothing.

There is no arousal looking at a woman, not because I think vagina is gross - I don't - it doesnt look like anything because there is NOTHING down there.

It just doesnt excite me ENOUGH to allow me to get off,
SO get off my ass
with all your phony ideas about homosexuality and what it means.

When I look at a vagina, something is missing.
There's nothing there. ERROR ISSUE WITH GENITALIA!
It's two floral, skin flaps.
It's missing something important.

AND THAT SOMETHING IS A BIG DICK!

Thats it. Thats being gay.

In a nutshell.
Let people bust a nut.

GUYS have penises, and those penises have to become erect to have
some enjoyment with them,
and then if they dont, you aint gettin nothin. (except a really awkward,
never wanna talk about it again encounter, sorry I had too much wine
and couldn't keep it up convo.)

Simple as that.

Were talking about DICK, but you dont have to be a dick to others
because your book says so.

This book says be nice.

Oh and by the way, the long standing complaint that homosexuality at
gay parades is too sexual... It has the word SEXUALITY in there.
Second of all, let people wear the unicorn boots and glittery boas all they
want. Its one week of the year.
Stop raining on peoples parade.

Thank you.

Oh my god
Laughs

*We just effortlessly bypassed over three thousand years of pain and
ignorance.*

You're FUCKING welcome.

We could have saved so much time,

and we could have saved SO MANY lives,
had that been said.

All that unthinkable SUFFERING because some man could ejaculate
onto a clam plate.
Pathetic. Absurd. Insane.

BUT HOMOSEXUALITY ISNT NATURAL!!!!

MAN....It's AS natural as waking up with morning wood poking out.
MAN....It's AS natural as getting an erection.

(we get a million of them everyday)

Listen. Even in my dreams, when I'm unconscious and not in control,
drooling on a pillow with my mouth hanging open,
there has never once been a naked woman pop up and do something
carnal. It's been sex with men all the way.
I'm not even conscious! My brain is, I'm passed the F out and still seeing
COCK. That's something far, far, FAR beyond the realm of daily human
control.

You can threaten me with hell until you face turns every shade of the
rainbow, quote every bible verse, speak in tongues,
but my dick still ain't moving an inch.

A SINGLE INCH.

And by the way - for the record - Sodom and Gomorrah was fake news.
That story is disgusting, imaginary, contradictory
and then the daughters end up fucking their own dad after getting him
drunk on wine.

But they say were the gross ones.

Gross.

They EVEN said the world would end once gay marriage was legal.
HAS IT?
The absolute fucking dramatics.

Remember when a legislator from my HOME state (Oklahomo)
said "Homosexuality is more dangerous to this nation than terrorist
attacks. "

*REALLY? Jesus Bleepin****** Christ.*
Yes, two men holding hands is more dangerous than people flying
planes into buildings and MURDERING
INNOCENTS?????????????????????????????????????
You people are mentally helpless, so HELP me God.

erases the rest of the chalkboard
deep sighs

Oh well, now you know.

I dont want to hear anything else about it, ever again.

You read this and think.. Ok, I think I finally get it (homosexuality) now.

How people managed to psychologically and socially abuse their own
children, making their offspring have deep seated issues FOR LIFE and
tell them they were worthless and destined for hell,
how parents and families looked down on their own biological creations
and relatives,
how people tortured each other into agonizing mental prisons -

That, I don't get.

"…, Well love the sinner, but hate the sin. "

NO.
Let's STOP ALL THE HATE.
NO MORE HATE, DAMNIT
IT'S NOT A SIN TO BE ALIVE!!!
PERIOD.
END OF STORY!

--

So we've just taken immeasurable pain, suffering, tears, poisonous
contemptuous, anger of the last several thousand years and
penultimately solved the problem in less than 50 pages.
Put it all into a cute, little pamphlet, for ya.
Didnt need to attack anyone, didnt need to insult their gods or their
sacred beliefs, (not too much)
didnt need to fight and argue.

Sweet Mother Mary, I let everyone else make a total fool of themselves,
fight and argue.
I may not be straight,
but now the record has been set straight.
Just put it on the table for all to see.
My work is done.

**Turns all the lights off, Leaves the classroom,*
*and quietly closes the heavy, old door behind me**

PART 2 - PART 2 IS THE PARTY
NOW SCREAM WITH ME

They lied their ass off about me,
Tonight get your ass in bed baby and lie with me
We'll only tell the truth,
(The naked truth)

Lets get into bed and have a conversation without any words (or clothes on)

They called me awful names
Call me only by my name,
But I wont be anyones booty call
Pick up that phone
Tonight I dont want to be alone
But Dont ask, Dont Telephone

I'm giving you a ring-a-ling,
Because tonight I've got an appointment
with yo ding-a-ling

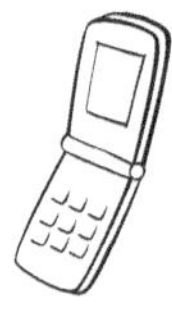 HELLO! PICK UP! TELLING YOUR OWN KIDS YOU HATE THEM

BECAUSE THEY ARE GAY ISNT A GOOD IDEA

THIS IS YOUR WAKE UP CALL

I don't need to come out,
but I need you to come closer
Come on
Let's touch and get over our sexual hangups,
I survived them all,
Not another gay man that was hanging in a closet
Now get on top of me,
My well hung man.

I'm calling you for a night in
and I'm calling this world OUT
I serve perfection,
they've never met someone who can so quickly talk about the
power of the erection
With some well placed puns,
Stick your pickle between my two buns.

Long gone are the days of the scholar,
Need a strong man to grab me by my collar

Since I can remember,
I've been PUSHING MYSELF
Need to find a man who will PULL ME CLOSE.

PECKER
Gregory Peck's Pecker,
My sweet prince,
when doves cry,
Get me spread Eagle,
I'll give you a real Birds eye View

Saw pictures of her Ovaries,
but was furiously rubbing my rooster
to pictures of his big peacock, instead

Show me your little white lizard, Come on
Dont be a chicken

I used to be the ugly ducking
Then I became the Swan Prince
Lets talk the Birds and the bees
Let me see the phallus that sits between your knees
The male member that both ejaculates, hardens and pees

One flew over the cuckoos nest,
Ill rattle their cages, and ruffle some feathers
These rhymes will be one for the ages
Now I go with the sages,
As wise as an owl
Pissing people off,

is a real hoot.

You'll never see me looking at a woman's hooters,
or doing night-time transactions with her cooter

Jim Crow
Right Wing, Left Wing
Let's get political, Lame ducks
Let's get physical
Let's get Levitcal, you stupid fucks
ILL MAKE THEM EAT CROW

I'm one of the very best,
Don't ya know?

(With well placed words,
I can make them hysterical)

My words will all fly over their heads,
after this book flies off the shelf!

The religious opinion of homosexuality
has TRULY always been one for the birds.

PRACTICING MY HOMOSEXUALITY
I don't need to practice much,
I can just wing it.

They'll never catch me,
Ill lead them on a wild goose chase.

Im about to cook their goose 

You thought you could take me down,
You're a silly goose,
And I'm holding the noose.

I can't help that I love to CHOKE a man's chicken.
Now get away from me with all your awful bible verses,
YOU BIRD BRAINS

CAW CAW

Hah- Hah.

3rd year RAVENKLAW

If you think Im done,
dont count your chickens before they hatch.
Don't care what you have to say, I ain't ever licking a snatch
THIS IS JUST THE FIRST BATCH.
Cooked this eggy up straight from scratch.

I'm watching you like a hawk right now.

I know what you think about me,
I know what you believe
because a little muslim birdy told me.

Jesus flipped over the tables in the temple,
I'll flip you off from the temple inside my head
Now I FLIP YOU THE BIRD.

Bird IS the word.
And the early bird really does get to suck on my worm.
I hope I make you people reading this cringe and SQUIRM.

I WANT your wood
I WANT your Pecker

If I fell asleep at work,
would that be considered my dream job?

If I sang in the shower,
would that be considered a soap Opera?

DANCE WITH ME, YOU STUPID MOTHERFUCKERS

Gluteus Maximus

A senile senate
Homo Erectus,
Republicans in Rome,
Democrats in Damascus,
Masc for Masc
Sit on my spear, and suck it
I'll wrestle you to the floor
and show you my backdoor

Amphetamines in the Amphitheater
The Crowd goes Roar
The Angry Lion bares his teeth for more
Blasphemous UPROAR
Doth Quoth the Raven,
Forevermore.

As one door closes,
their mind closes another
CLOSE MINDED
WEARING NO CLOTHES
YOU THINK IM TALKING ABOUT MY BODY BUT
ILL SHOW YOU MIND.

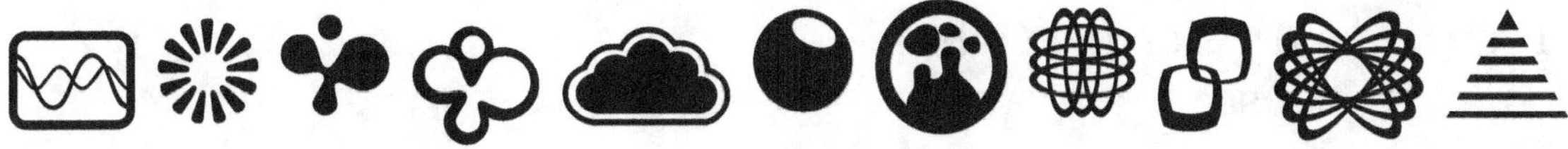

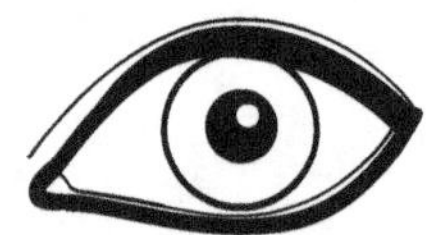

An eye for an eye,
He pulled out - of what is known as - my brown eye
and finished near my Blue Eye
It damn nearly gave me Pink eye,
I know you're rolling your eyes,
I know you're giving me the stink eye
I'll fight you, give you a black eye
(in the USA, might not be safe if you're a black guy)
IN AMERICA, OH SAY CAN YOU SEE
I've got all eyes on me
Men are my eye candy
You killed 2many of MY kind,
CANT YOU SEE
So I'll kill you with kindness
I'll show you how to TURN THE OTHER CHEEK
THE OTHER BUTT CHEEK
KISS MY ASS BECAUSE THIS ONE IS AN EYE FOR EYE
I bet this book was a real eye opener
I've been watching you
with eyes in the back of my head
Talking about private things
In the public eye
TIRED OF ALL THE BULLSHIT
SO I HIT A PERFECT BULLSEYE
Im a bat out of hell,
But I can cuss someone out and not even bat an eye
Eye of the Hurrican,
Eye of the Tiger
Cat Eyes,
Now feast your eyes on my next move.
I can keep going
for as long as the eye can see.
Will I ever truly forgive them?
Eye don't think so.

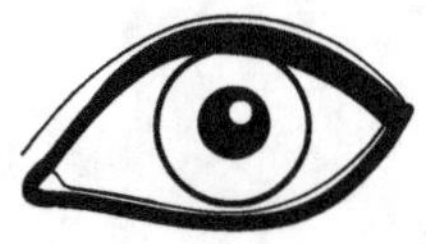

Private eye,
I've got my eyes on your privates
DICKTECTIVE,
Let's get to the bottom of this.

Let me inspect
what has now (obviously) become erect.

UNDER COVER LOVERS,
GET UNDER THESE COVERS
IVE GOT OVER THREE THOUSAND YEARS OF BULLSHIT TO FLY PAST
WEVE GOT A LOT OF GROUND TO COVER

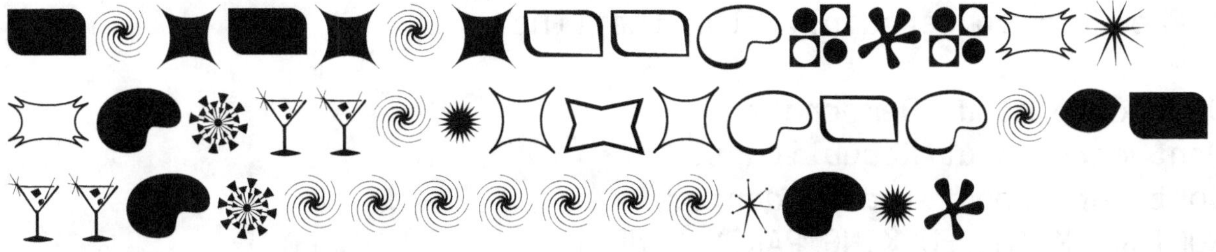

Line by Line,
Standing in the frontlines,
Writing this on a deadline,
Going as fast as I can before time makes my heart flatline,
Making my family mad,
OOPS! THERE GOES MY DOWRY FROM MY BLOODLINE
HERE COMES THE NEXT PUNCHLINE
Im trying my best,
THROW ME A LIFELINE
Did this in under 1 week,
Published on a timeline
My writing is top of the line,
I love naked men's ding dongs
and thats just the BOTTOM LINE

Leaving writing behind, for science
Social science for Pure sciences,
I'm already way on down the line
Will I have any more books coming down the pipeline?
Dont know,
but I'm almost there to the finish line
This isnt my line of work,
I dont like being in the line of fire,
much less their THREATS of a lake of fire

I've done a knockout job,
wrote it all hook line and sinker
Some of it was serious,
Some of it was funny,
So Whose line is it anyway?

Is he on drugs,
Is he snorting lines?
I know how to certainly blur the line.

Dont care about Democrats,
Dont care about Republicans,
Dont care about Independents,
WONT WALK THE FUCKING PARTY LINE
MY MESSAGE IS A
POWERLINE

Wrote it all Offline,
and Had it published ONLINE

EVEN THOUGH I AM GAY
I MOVE ONLY IN STRAIGHT LINES

We're already coming to the end of the line
This was.
The.
Storyline.

Keep your eyes on me,
Someday I'll be making the HEADLINES.

This reality is a MADHOUSE
So much pent up anger
residing in the penthouses
Is there a disturbance in your residence?
Write it
with the cadence
of dissidence
Distract them, while I clean up all the semen strains evidence
With one of his nuts in my mouth,
I'm a nutcase living in a
NUTHOUSE
Finally could get married,
Take me down to the courthouse,
They were all SO full of shit,
In and out
of the Outhouse
Catty words,
I've put them all in the doghouse

Not another gay man,
You won't catch me in any bathhouse
Without a publisher
I don't need to sign with randomhouse or penguinhouse

Working in a little restaurant
In the front of house,
Trying to save up enough
to finally leave the poorhouse
Made this meal, Homemade,
After this book,
Baby, I got it made.
Sign the tax documents + Make me your spouse
They all ingloriously lied,

Now let's get gloriously laid.
LAY THE PIPE DOWN ON ME, BABY
Check my plumbing,
Oh God,
I think I'm comi---

Changing their tune,
I'll have them all absolutely humming.

These words are filthy,
But someday I'll be filthy rich
Rich enough to own a boathouse,
I'll be the man of the house
And that's the way the cookie crumbles
LOL It's Toll House
I'm an angel from hell,
Burning down this MOTHAFUCKIN house

garage, living room, attic, basement, bathroom, bedroom,
laundry room, diving room,
MASTURBATION IN THE MASTERBEDROOM
A place to fornicate for the aroused Groom and Groom
Tv Room, Staircase, Study
Come a little closer, buddy

That's enough out of you, Buddy
NOW GET THE FUCK OUT OF MY HOUSE

Through all of that heavy darkness,
I had the strength, willpower to be a lighthouse.
I WILL FOREVER BE A POWERHOUSE

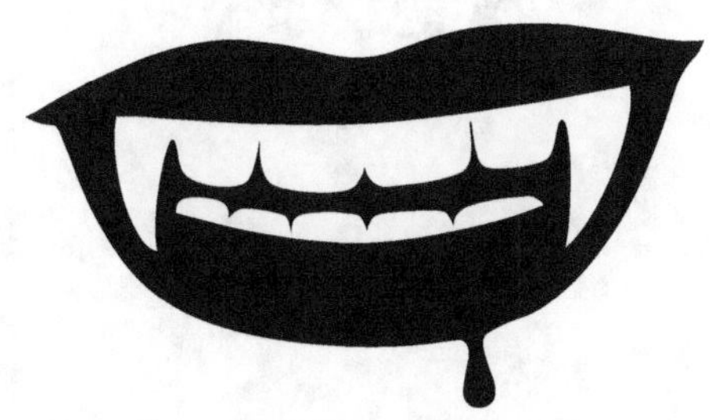

Watch out!
That cocksucker is a bloodsucker
He wants to suck on your ------------ blood, bud
He's a tramp, He's a vamp
This is the time stamp,
With the bookmark of the beast.

Dracula with a wig becomes Dragula
Crazy like Caligula
Cookin Trouble up in the kitchen
Get the Spatulas

Now get the eggs,
And open up your legs.

BITE ME

Their words about gays really bug me,
Turn on the windshield wiper
Abrahamic, Middle Eastern Viper
American Sniper,
Dressed Sharp, you'll be the sharpshooter
You might not be all that straight, but you're a real straight-
shooter
Right to bare arms, now let me bare my legs and my butt HAH!
Come in guns a blazin, talking about reproduction with the sex

pistols

They say you bite the pillow,

tonight they'll all be biting the bullet. 

Bop it, Twist it, Pull it!
Yin-Yang, Let me GRIP your Hairy Wang.

Smoked 2 much pot and lost the plot
And When I lost my mind,
I was the gay man
they tried to keep restrained in a straight jacket
I escaped
I won my victory
after they talked ALL that smack, lettuce get in the sack,
and I'll play with your sac, toss my salad from the back.
I'm a total wisecrack,
never been one to hold back
Obsessed with the future,
I don't look spend my time looking back.
Can handle them,
don't worry about the push back
I'll flash them
while I have these psychological flashbacks
Get the KODAK
Wrote this in a paperback.
Like music to my hears,
My first book was titled "A sodomite's soundtrack." (ASS)
But I changed it to the Direction of your Erection,
Because I liked the playback.
Im an artist, drawing it out now,
but this one has no drawbacks.
I can safely say I kicked their asses,

and can now enjoy a nice financial kickback.
Years ago, I killed the blonde,
and since I was 15 - my hair has been kept a dark, jet black.
Never been afraid to speak up and stand up,
You might wanna standback,
I've done something I can't take back,
And I know there is no going back.

No matter what happens, going forward,
from every edge of defeat
I've got the resources and the resilience
to bounce back.

Won't let anyone ride my coatails,
you won't be getting an intellectual piggyback
I've been coached how to conduct myself,
you bitches can all give me five and do a jumpingjack
Like a butterfly, like a bee
YellowJack
Dont worry about their negativity,
I've already gotten enough positive feedback
Truth is, I'm talking about sex
but I ain't no nymphomaniac
This was just my angle of attack.
Aquarius, Water carrier
11th sign of the zodiac.
Often thought as a megalomanic.
But Always a brainiac.
Pick up an almanac
I can go my own way,
off the beaten track
You've been beaten, NOW BEAT IT
I'm leaving English literature
to work behing the scenes in science,
there is my biofeedback

Yes I know what they think about me
and
I don't care.
I only want to become a millionaire.
and see my face in the pages of Vanity fair.
I'm a social climber,
and this is just the first step up of that infamous stair.

Put your hardware inside my software
I questioned their ideas
With this brief questionnaire
They were all full of hot air,
but I was capable of walking on sunshine, and walking on air.
They showed me hate,
but writing was always my first love affair
I want everyone to hear this,
From Denmark to Delaware
and even farther,
Elsewhere.
America has a lot of problems right now,
from tolerance to healthcare
everyone acts like a belligerent child,
They need to go to daycare, but nobody can afford childcare
The American Dream
is sometimes a Nationalistic Nightmare

Here we are, Somewhere
Where are we going, Nowhere
Where is Everyone at, Everywhere
Their, They're and There
It'll all be okay... There, there, there
This was fun,
Until next time,
Take care.

Did you see what I did there? X-RAY
This 1 was X-Rated
I'm not an X-man,
just a gay man,
Gambit was always my favorite man,
and this was my actual gamble.

On, shall I ramble.
Leave their ideas in a real shamble,
to work against me,
they'll have to be quicker than me and scramble,
Now scram,
This is just the preamble.

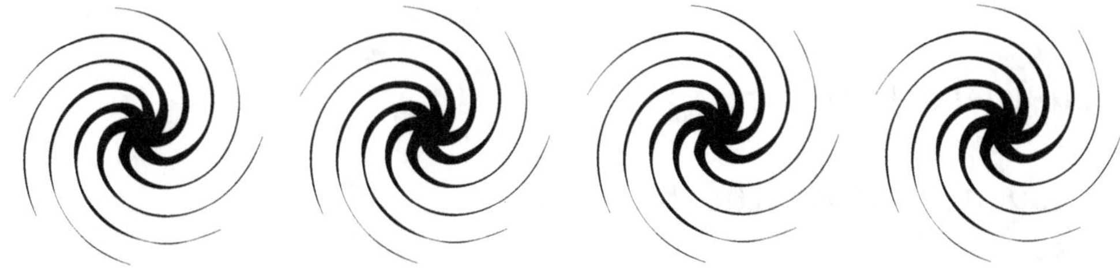

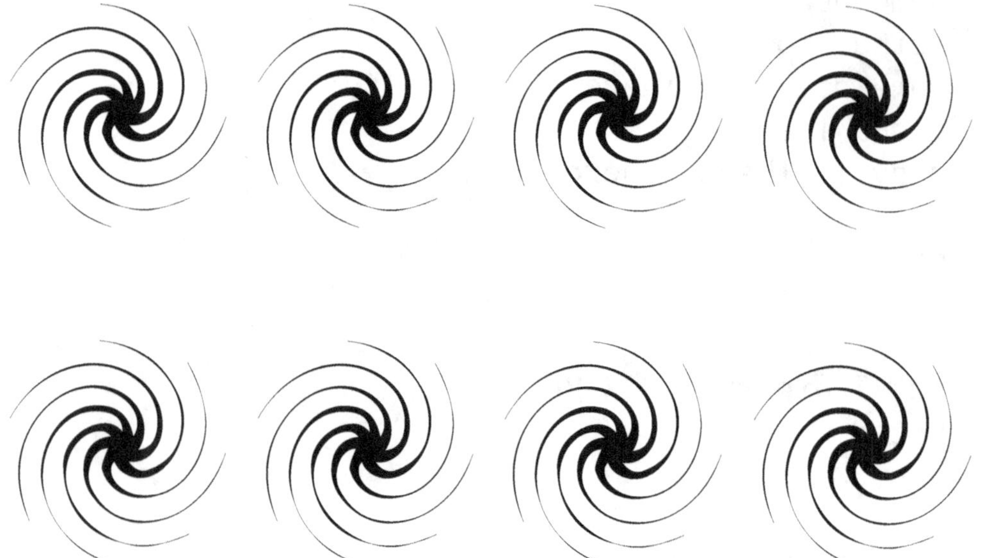

I've taken a difficult subject that people couldn't explain in thousands and thousands of books.
I did this - effortlessly - in less than 30 pages.
The beekeepers and gatekeepers of the literary world can suck a fat one.

Lastly, King Solomon - from the bible - had 700 wives and THREE HUNDRED concubines (pretty semen vessels and you know it)
and you jerkoffs… you jerkoffs actually tried to stop me from having ONE husband.
ONE HUSBAND, BUT HE CAN HAVE 1,000 WIVES.

Rips hair out
I'm going to La-la-La-Lose it!

I really hate you all. What the hell. LOL.
Of the same sex,
but this is NOT the same old STORY
of Adam and <u>Steve</u>,
Could have saved this world all the time and trouble,

by saying my willy just won't get **HARD** or **BIG**

for <u>Eve.</u>

The. Fucking. End.

OH!
There actually is one more crucial piece of data to be added.
Something maybe even more important.

Because I'm not taking off my pants and showing you my wiener,
Since A. How awkward, my God and B. I'm not a porn star and
THAT's not my vocation/occupation, but there is one actual
thing that WILL convince you. At least it should beyond a
shadow of a doubt. Something less carnal and easier to speak
about.

It's the voice. <u>Gay voice</u>. It's very real.

You know EXACTLY what I'm talking about.

Almost every homosexual has it, some to greater and lesser
degrees.

We're not choosing to sound like that.

DEFINITELY. NOT.

WHO WOULD WANT TO SOUND LIKE THAT?????????????????

I've wanted to rip my voice box out since I heard the horrid,
dreaded gay voice it came with. But I'm stuck with it for life.

Sweet Jesus, it's terrible.

Unless vocal modification becomes real in the future (PLEASE)

Anyway, so you don't need to see my junk, just listen to a gay
man TALK. There is something waiting to be unlocked there
eventually by scientists, I just know it.

I'm trapped beneath layers of that infamous gay voice, acting
as constant interference in my communication.

It's a final, definitive, incontrovertible proof that
homosexuality is natural.

I may not like my speaking voice, but the voice you're hearing
inside here is 100% pure. I can change the world with it.

Winks at the audience

The Real, Final End.